MW01097343

Wood Pallets for Beginners

15 DIY Household Projects to Reuse Wood Pallets

Table of Content

Introduction 4

Chapter 1 - Wood Pallet Wall...6

    Materials 6

    Directions...6

Chapter 2 - Wine Rack...8

    Materials 8

    Directions...8

Chapter 3 - Planter...10

    Materials 10

    Directions...10

Chapter 4 - Decorative Tray...12

    Materials 12

    Directions...12

Chapter 5 - Electronics Shelf 14

    Materials 14

    Directions...14

Chapter 6 - Bike Rack...16

    Materials 16

    Directions...16

Chapter 7 - Herb Trough...17

    Materials 17

    Directions...17

Chapter 8 - Spice Rack...18

    Materials 18

    Directions...18

Chapter 9 - Compost Bin 20

    Materials 20

    Directions..20

Chapter 10 - Desktop Planter 22

    Materials 22

    Directions..22

Chapter 11 - See Thru Birdhouse 24

    Materials 24

    Directions..24

Chapter 12 - Spoon Shelf 26

    Materials 26

    Directions..26

Chapter 13 - Wine Box..29

    Materials 29

    Directions..29

Chapter 14 - Bat Box 31

    Materials 31

    Directions..31

Chapter 15 - Raised Bed Garden..34

    Materials 34

    Directions..34

Conclusion 36

Introduction

We all want a home that's well-decorated, functional, and personal, but not everyone can spend a fortune ordering expensive pieces of furniture from catalogs, and some would like to create a home that's unique to their personality. There's no better way to do all that than to create your own furniture, decorations, and functional pieces in your home from wood pallets. Pallets are everywhere. They're a huge part of the shipping industry, but if you're worried about where your pallet may have been, you can always order a new one from a manufacturer.

If you're going to go with used pallets, then here are some things you want to keep an eye out for.

Number one, you want to make sure the pallet has a logo stamped on it. Not all pallets will have one because it could have been rubbed off during shipping, and stamping pallets is not always mandatory depending on which country it's coming from. These are the following codes for the treatment code:

- *MB: Methyl Bromide*

- *HT: Heat Treated*

- *KD: Kiln Dried*

- *DB: Debarked*

Heat treated pallets are made in the United States or Canada and undergo a pest control that's known as heat treating. This entails heating the pallet to a core temperature of one hundred and thirty-three degrees Fahrenheit for softwood to one hundred and forty degrees Fahrenheit for a hardwood pallet for thirty minutes. These are not harmful to a person's health and are safe if not treated with anything else.

Kiln dried wood is to reduce the moisture content of the wood. That means it will control fungal growth, warping, and other quality control features. These boards don't normally reach temperatures that the heat treated boards do, but it's enough to keep them safe.

Methyl bromide fumigation is a powerful pesticide that has been linked to ozone layer depletion and is harmful to human health. This is banned in Canada, but it's used in other countries and poses a health risk. Do not use this as firewood or in a craft project as it's harmful to your health!

Debarked boards are just as they sound. It means the wood was debarked using the IPPC regulations. This doesn't indicate the safety of a pallet, so be sure to check for the other codes mentioned.

With that being said, you can now begin your journey of creating awesome projects with pallets!

Chapter 1 - Wood Pallet Wall

If you want to add some zing to your bedroom wall or maybe you want to make a living room fireplace look rustic, break apart some wood pallets and start attaching them to your wall! It's actually pretty simple and makes your room look cozy and cottage-like.

Materials

- Safety Gloves

- Nail gun

- Pallets

- Nails

- Wood Glue

- Wood Stain

Note: The amount of pallets you'll need will depend on the size of your wall, as will the amount of nails you'll need. Be sure to measure the wall and estimate how much wood you'll need to complete the project before beginning. It's better to purchase more and have some left over for a smaller project rather than not having enough, so overestimate.

Directions

1. Take apart the pallets gently, attempting not to break apart the top and bottom pieces that you'll be using on the wall.

2. Prepare the wall through coating it with some primer or at least cleaning it. After the wall has been prepared, measure to see how many pallets you'll need.

3. Apply some wood glue to one side of the pallet piece and glue it to the wall, beginning at the top or lower right or left corner.

4. Use the nail gun in the four corners of the pallet to keep it in place. Repeat these first four steps until the entire wall has been covered.

5. If you have any gaps on the edges of the wall, measure that space and cut some pieces to fit so that you cover the entire wall.

6. If you want a rustic look, cover up the nails with some wood putty and wait twenty-four hours before staining the entire wall.

Chapter 2 - Wine Rack

This is a simple, one bottle wine rack that holds glasses, too.

Materials

- (2) 4.75"x43.5" Pallet Boards

- (2) 4.75"x4" Pallet Boards

- Black Paint

- Table Saw

- Sander

- Drill

- Clamps

Directions

1. Cut all the pieces of wood to size and sand them. Just sand to get off the dirt for now and worry about a finer sanding later.

2. Make a hole with a 38mm drill bit so that it will fit almost any bottle. Use the 25mm drill bit to make the large opening in the center of the bottom piece and then use a 15mm drill bit to make the opening to the larger hole so you can slide the glasses in.

3. Pre-drilling any holes makes the assembly a lot easier. In addition, you want to use some clamps to get it together properly. Use some wood glue to glue the four pieces together, making sure the bottom piece is on the bottom and facing out properly to slide in the glasses, and the opening for

the bottle is on the side you'd like it on. Then clamp them together and allow them to sit overnight to cure.

4. Before you paint, you need to sand off the entire piece now. Use 60 to 120, then 180 to 240 to get a smooth finish. You want to sand until there is a soft, silky feeling when you touch the wood.

5. You can use any type or color of paint you want on your wine rack. This tutorial uses black paint, but you can use another color or even stain the pieces to give it a cozier look.

6. Wait twenty-four hours after you finish he piece and then hang it on the wall with a few hooks and enjoy!

Chapter 3 - Planter

This planter is good for a small tree or a large tomato plant and can be used indoors or outdoors.

Materials

- 4 Pieces of Pallet Wood The Same Length (For the Legs)

- 8 Side Bars (Make Sure They're The Width of the Planter)

- Nails

- Nail Gun

- Side Panel Pieces

Directions

1. Cut the four legs the height you want your planter to be, and then cut the eight sidebars to the width you want your planter to be. Then disassemble the rest of the pallet if you haven't already and set aside planks for your sides.

2. Build two matching sides. The lower side piece shouldn't touch the ground so that you avoid water. You should end up with two legs with two sidebars in between for each side, one sidebar at the top and one at the bottom on the inside.

3. Then use the remaining side bars to attach your two sides together to make a cube.

4. Use nails for the sides as you attach them to the sidebars, one nail on the bottom and one on the top. You don't need a lot because they're not load bearing.

5. Once you're done, make a cube to put on the top as a frame to hide any shorter or longer pieces of siding.

6. Put an old bin or a bucket in the center that's low enough to be hidden by the planter and put a plant in it!

Chapter 4 - Decorative Tray

You won't need much to make this decorate tray, but it'll end up looking like something you bought from an expensive art gallery by the time you're finished!

Materials

- A Dismantled Pallet

- 1 ¾" Nails

- Wood Glue

- Dark Stain

- 2 Cabinet Door Hinges

- Gloves

- Petroleum Jelly

- Spray Paint

- Paper Towels

- Foam Brushes

- Screw Driver

- Drill Bit

- Sander

Directions

1. Disassemble your pallet and make sure you have three unbroken deck boards. Cut out two thirteen inches and four twenty-two inch deck boards.

Some dent or imperfections will add some character, but make sure the boards are not broken. Sand the rough edges and the top until you reach your desired smoothness.

2. Add a good amount of wood glue between the two thirteen inch boards on the edges where they will go together and add some to the four twenty-two inch boards. Secure them together and allow them to dry.

3. With a sponge brush, add a little stain with a random pattern. Once it's been absorbed, smear the petroleum jelly on the parts you want to stay visible.

4. Now spray paint your tray and allow it to dry completely. You might need a few coats to get it covered. Once it's dry, wipe it with some paper towel to get rid of the petroleum jelly and you'll see the dark stain showing through.

5. Now, add the hardware to complete the look. Use some cabinet door hardware and attach them on either side of the shorter ends of the tray so you can easily pick it up.

Chapter 5 - Electronics Shelf

Are you tired of your entertainment center not being able to hold all the electronic devices you have for your television? Does your child need something in their room to hold their equipment but you don't want to purchase an expensive entertainment center for them? Then make an electronics shelf!

Materials

- 1 Pallet

- Screws and Drill

- ½" Thick Scrap Piece of Wood

- Sander

- Shelves or Boards

- Shelf Brackets

Directions

1. Sand off any rough edges and dust off the cobwebs and dirt.

2. Choose the height you prefer your shelves to be and then screw the brackets onto the pallet. If the holes don't line up, then use some extra-long screws to reach the vertical two by fours.

3. You need to locate a stud to screw the pallet into on the wall. Due to trim at the bottom of your wall, use a small piece of scrap wood the same depth as your trim and put it between the pallet and the wall before you screw it into the stud. This keeps it standing straight.

4. Screw on the shelves. Weave the cords through the pallet for your electronics and plug them in!

Chapter 6 - Bike Rack

Bike racks can be expensive, but using two pallets and attaching them together makes an awesome bike rack you can paint or even just finish with some wood stain to make it look chic!

Materials

- 1 Pallet with Thinner Boards

- 1 Pallet with Larger Boards

Directions

1. The pallet with the thinner boards is the one you will be leaning against the wall because the narrower slots will hold the bike wheels. The other pallet is going to go upside down.

2. For the pallet that's sitting on the ground, you want a little more wiggle-room to line up the wheels to fit into the vertical slots. You can do this through setting the pallet with the boards down. This provides a little 'well' for the wheels and gives you a cross-brace to keep the wheel from rolling out of place. Note that you need a little distance from the wall and the bottom pallet so you can lean the top pallet against the wall to keep it steady.

3. Put your bikes on!

Chapter 7 - Herb Trough

You may have made the planter already, but herb troughs are a little different. This is more like a feed trough design so you can put many more herbs in the planter without having to use too much dirt.

Materials

- 2-3 Pallets

- Wood Screws

- Cordless Drill

Directions

1. Measure out the size you want your herb box to be. A good place to start would be three feet long by a foot wide. This will allow you to put in plenty of herb plants!

2. Now measure out a frame. You'll need four legs attached together by a three foot by one-foot frame. Then put another frame on the top.

3. Now attach your sides lengthwise. You can put a plastic liner on the inside of the box in order to keep the wood protected and make your box last longer.

4. Fill it up with dirt and plant your herbs!

Chapter 8 - Spice Rack

Are you tired of your small spice rack and you'd like something a little larger? Then make a spice rack out of a pallet!

Materials

- 1 Pallet

- Sander

- Wood Glue

Directions

1. First you want to dismantle and lay out the spice rack pattern with your pallet. To dismantle the pallet, stand it on its side and use a saw to cut through the nails on either end. This lets you use the entire length of the board without splitting the back or the board. When it's dismantled, lay out the boards that will work for your space where you want to put the rack. Cut the boards as little as possible if you have a large space. Know that some boards will be different widths and might need to be used in another project. Sand all the boards on all sides before you move on.

2. Now, use some wood glue to connect the four sides of the rack together. Due to not wanting to cut the boards too much, you'll need to use the full length of the pallet boards for the sides and only cut the ones that you will use lengthwise. Wood glue will keep everything together just fine as long as you clamp it and you let it sit overnight to cure.

3. When the back and the frame are together, insert the boards you'll be using for the shelves and glue them from the sides. The measurements for

the height of the shelves will be based on the different heights of spices, or you can put the shelves all in at an even distance.

4. Before you hang the rack, you might want to run the sander over it again just to get rid of any glue pieces or any little splintered pieces that might have come up throughout your process. If you don't know where the wood came from that you're using, you might want to spray it with a bleach solution to make it safe for the kitchen.

Chapter 9 - Compost Bin

Compost bins are excellent additions to any garden, whether it's a vegetable or flower garden. To create a really easy compost bin you can start adding kitchen scraps to right away, just grab yourself four pallets and get started with this tutorial!

Materials

- 4 Pallets
- 14 Gauge Wire
- Hinges
- Latch

Directions

1. Begin by cutting the wire to eighteen inch long pieces and strap the side and back pallets together through twisting the wire tight. Don't overdo it or the wire will snap. Two pieces of wire twisted one each corner should be fine.

2. Put a landscape pole on the hinge side of the bin. The pallets are not light so you need some support for the door pallet. Hammer the pole into the ground about a foot.

3. Add the hinges to the hinge side. Put a spacer on the bottom with some leftover landscaping pole and attach that with screws. This allows some ventilation for the compost because all the other sides are sitting on the ground.

4. Add a latch if you want to keep any children or animals out of your bin.

5. If you live in a dry climate, you need moisture in your bin to keep it composting. So add some plastic to the top to keep it moist and warm inside.

Chapter 10 - Desktop Planter

Does your desktop need a little green on it, but you don't want to spend too much green to get it? Then use some scrap pieces of pallet from your other projects to make yourself a little desktop planter!

Materials

- Pallet Pieces

- Plastic Cups

- Nails

- Wood Glue

- Potting Mix

- The Plant

- Hammer

- Saw

Directions

1. It's as easy as measuring out the wood and gluing it together. Let's use the example of a four inch by four-inch planter. Measure the width of the wood and subtract it from four inches. Sand the pieces and measure out the bottom.

2. Glue the wood together and nail on the bottom. Then use a little wood putty between the pieces if you want a more contemporary design, and sand it again.

3. You can then paint it any color you wish or leave it unfinished for a rustic look.

4. Put the plastic cup inside and put a plant in it!

Chapter 11 - See Thru Birdhouse

Have you ever wondered what it was like to look inside a bird house while the birds were actually using it? Well, now you can with this see-through birdhouse that features a screen at the back so you can hang it near a window in order to look inside!

Materials

- Saw

- Pallet planks

- Drill

- Hammer

- Hole saw kit

- Ruler

- Nails

- Pen

Directions

1. To make the window, you'll want to take the cover off an old CD case and bend the edges forward very carefully. There'll be a snap and then you'll have a clean break. Sand down the edges to make it smooth and get rid of any sharp edges. Then use a drill to make a small hole in every corner.

2. Use some pallet planks to make the birdhouse. The plank you'll want to use should be six inches wide and half an inch thick. Use a ruler to mark the wood at five, ten, fifteen, and twenty inches. This gives you four six by

five-inch pieces for the walls. Then measure and cut the front panel of the house so that it fits within the interior of the walls when it's put together. It should be four and a half inches squared.

3. For this birdhouse, we will be making the hole one and a half inches wide, which is best for small birds. Mark the center point of the two adjacent sides of the four and a half inch squared piece. Draw a line between these two points. Make a vertical line from corner to corner to make a cross. Measure one and a half inches down from your horizontal line to make a second line. Then make two more vertical lines three-quarters of an inch from   the   center   vertical   line.

You should now have a box. Figure out the center of the box by making an X from corner to corner. Now you have the center point of the bird house entrance. Use a drill and a one and a half inch hole saw to cut out your hole.

4. This step of the process is optional. If you want to add a perch to the nest box, then drill a hole under the entrance and put a small piece of dowel inside with some wood glue.

5. Assemble the walls around the entrance so that the birdhouse is six inches deep. Use nails to put the wood together, four to five for every side, in an overlapping pattern so that it fits around the entrance. Then secure the plastic window on the back.

6. Hang your birdhouse in front of a window and wait for the birds to make a nest!

Chapter 12 - Spoon Shelf

Spoon shelves can be used just about anywhere in the home, but they make a statement when your guests enter and hang their jackets on silver spoons in your foyer. If you haven't guessed already, a spoon shelf is actually a piece of wood with spoons underneath that have been cut and bent into the shape of a hook. Look for some fancy, old-fashioned spoons at your local thrift shop to give this project a pop!

Materials

- 2 Wide Pallet Boards

- 3 Spoons

- Miter Saw

- Sand Paper

- Sander

- Brad Nailer

- Screw Driver

- ½" Screws

Directions

1. First let's begin with the pallet. You're going to need two of the wider boards and one side board. Cut the first board to thirty-four inches. The second board is going to be at twenty-eight inches. Now let's cut the side piece. You want the shape of the side piece to be noticeable on the shelf so measure three inches from the curve and cut the end off. Then put the piece up against the board and mark how long it should be.

2. Then sand the ends of all the pieces to make them smooth but don't sand them too much because you want a rustic look! Make sure you sand the edges and get any splinters off. Then dry fit the pieces together to make sure the look is good. Do a three-inch overhang on either side.

3. Use the brad nailer for this next step. Nail the base first and turn the back upside down and use a table to line it all up. Nail it through the back of the board into the side piece. Four nails should be good. Then lay the shelf on its back and line up your top. Remember the three-inch overhang on the sides! Nail it to the top into the side piece and then into the back piece. You're almost finished!

4. Now you want to stain it. You don't have to be too careful with this. Just get it on there with a rag or an old paint brush. Once you have it all covered, wipe off any excess with a clean rag. While the stain is drying, you can begin with the spoons.

5. You want to use old spoons from a thrift store and not your good silverware! Begin by laying the spoons face down on a hard surface. Be careful about the surface because this will mark up a wood table. Start at the middle of the spoon and work out toward the end. If you pound in one spot too much, you'll have to turn it over and pound from the other side, which will seriously weaken the metal. You want the spoon completely flat and bent away from the handle.

6. Now bend the handle so the design is facing outside of the bend. That way you'll see it when you hang it! For most, you'll be able to bend them with your hands but find something round so it's a smooth bend.

7. Use a drill press to put two one eight inch holes in the spoons. It's pretty simple, just drill one on top and one on the bottom of the face of the spoon. After the holes have been drilled, be sure to remove any metal shards with a file.

8. Now just screw on the screws with a half inch stainless steel screw. First measure between the two side pieces to find the center. Then screw in a center spoon. Then measure four inches away from the center and put in another spoon. The same on the other side.

Chapter 13 - Wine Box

This wine box makes the perfect carrier for a holiday gift to the in-laws, or cousins, or aunt, or whomever! This is a simple, elegant box with beautiful décor on it that will blow your receiver's mind away.

Materials

- Pallet Wood Planks

- Saw

- Planer

- Sander

- Router Saw

- Wood Glue

Directions

1. Gather some thirty-nine inch by five and a half inch pallet boards. Plan your layout so that the cuts will get rid of any nail holes.

2. Cut the boards down to a rough length. You'll be cutting them down to finish size later on. Basically, cut off the ends and the center section where the nail holes are.

3. Now plane down to a quarter inch thickness with the planer.

4. Take all four side pieces and rip them to five and a half inches and the top and bottom to five inches.

5. The long side boards should be cut to sixteen inches and the short sides should be cut to four and a half inches.

6. This is where things get a little fancy. You're going to need a quarter inch straight cut bit on the router table to a depth of a quarter of an inch. Bo the short end sides will get a quarter inch dado that will be a quarter of an inch from the edge. The longer sides will get a stopped dado on the bottom and a dado that ends on one side and through on the other side to all for the top to slide in and out.

7. Take one of the shorter pieces and cut off a quarter inch strip above your dado and save it. This will be glued to the top to act as a handle yet still keep the original lines of your box.

8. Now it's time to build your fancy wine box! Be sure to apply enough wood glue to every joint. Use some brad nails to help hold the box together until the glue dries. Even though it has butt joints, the box will be strong enough.

9. Now slide the top panel into the dado in the box and mark where you need to cut it. Then take the top panel and use the miter saw to chop off one end. Take the small piece that cut off the shorter side panel and glue that on like a little pull.

10. Now do some light sanding. You don't want to take the wood down too far or you'll get rid of that rustic look of the pallet boards. Sand the edges to get rid of any little splinters and slide the top panel on and sand the end so it's flush while it's in the closed position.

11. Now you can decorate the box with anything you want! If you're talented, you can paint the top, or you can use a photo transfer from an inkjet printer   and   apply   a   little   lacquer   to   it.

Chapter 14 - Bat Box

Bats are actually very beneficial little critters to the environment, and if you have a problem in the attic, you can easily move them outside with one of these neat little projects! Just find a sunny area on the south side of your home and be sure to close off any areas that lead back into your home.

Materials

- Untreated Pallets

- Pry Bar

- Hammer

- Screws

- Drill

- Caulk

- Wood Stain

- Varnish

- Shingles

- Stapler

Directions

1. Be sure you're using a pallet that hasn't been chemically treated. Look for HT on it to make sure its heat treated because you don't want the bats becoming intoxicated.

2. Dismantling your pallet might be more of a challenge than you think. Not all of them are created equal, and some of them can be made for extremely heavy hauls. You'll most likely have to end up cutting off the ends of the planks because they'll be damaged by using the crowbar on them. That's okay. Just take your time and find spots you can pry on.

3. You'll want to plan out the box according to where you're located. You'll want to look up bats in your location and what they prefer. This tutorial is going to be for the Little Brown Bat since they're common. This is also a box for a colder climate as the bats will need less ventilation in order to stay warm. Cut the planks to twenty inches by twenty-four-inch lengths, with the center planks being nineteen and a quarter inch in length.

4. Bats have very strong feet and claws, but they will still need a little roughness to get a grip on their landing strip. Secure your plank with some clamps and make a score on the wood every half inch or so with a circular saw blade adjusted to an eighth-inch thickness. The planks will be uneven, so just adjust the blade a little lower for warps in the wood. Score the parts that will be interior surfaces and score the center planks on both sides.

5. Use a small diameter bit to predrill any nail holes so you don't split all the wood you just prepared.

6. Now for the assembling. Clamp down your center planks with the grooves on both sides facing each other. Then nail down the side piece and leave a quarter inch gap at the top to share heat across the center barrier. Turn it around and nail the other side piece, and be sure to check to make sure the angled roof cuts are on the same end. Then nail the roof on the top and be sure it's flush with the back planks. Now nail on the front and back planks.

7. Caulk any cracks and holes if you live in a colder climate. If you live in a warm climate, then be sure *not* to caulk cracks and holes because the bats need more ventilation. Wait for the caulk to dry before you paint or stain the exterior part of the box. For a colder climate, use a dark stain to absorb

more heat from the sunlight. Be sure the paint is water based, and then varnish the wood after the stain has dried.

8. When you install your bat box, you want to be near a known bat nesting area. The box needs to be at least twenty feet off the ground or as high as a ladder will take you. It should be about a thousand feet from any known open water sources. You need a wide area around the box that's not obstructed, and if you live in the north, the box should be in full sunlight to get as much heat as possible in the winter.

Chapter 15 - Raised Bed Garden

You've already seen a tutorial for a herb box, but this is a much larger raised bed garden that you can put pepper, tomato, eggplant, and so many other larger vegetables into! If you want to get fancy, you can even attach a trellis to the side for your climbing plants.

Materials

- Pallets

- Crow Bar

- Circular Saw

- Sander

- Nail Gun

- Nails

- Trim

Directions

1. You'll want to look for pallets that are free or low-cost because you'll need a few of them to complete this project. If you're near a warehouse business, just stop in and ask them if you can take a few pallets. Chances are they'll be ecstatic to get rid of them. Just make sure they're heat treated and not chemically treated if you're growing any vegetables you'll be consuming. The newer pallets are usually heat treated, but some of the older ones were treated with chemicals and should be avoided.

2. Once you have the pallets home, you'll want to tear them apart into usable pieces. This is harder than it sounds. You'll want a crowbar or pry bar to

gently each the boards apart. Or you can use a saws-all in order to get them apart by cutting the nails. That's the easiest way. Once the boards are off, you should have some notched out two by fours.

3. Now you need to cut your planks for the raised bed. It's best to use a circular saw for this process. Cut the wood into three or four-inch strips. Cut the boards down to thirty-six-inch pieces. You'll end up with three and four-inch boards that are thirty-six inches long.

4. Now you need to cut six fourteen inch pieces from the two by fours that came from the pallets. These are going to be the four corners of your raised bed and for the center of the boxes.

5. Now you need to group the planks together and lay them out. The raised bed will be a foot tall so you'll need to get a few three or four-inch pieces to make twelve inches. The sides will consist of four side sections and the two ends, so you'll need six groups of boards that will get you to twelve inches tall. You'll then lay out your six fourteen inch pieces of two by four to connect the corners and the centers of the long sides.

6. Once everything has been laid out, you'll then begin joining your side boards to the supports. Every side section is going to overlap the center of the support halfway and be secured with nails. The support will extend below the bottom and the corners. This gives it a little stability because you'll be putting it into the ground a bit. Use two nails per board and be sure to predrill the holes to avoid splitting the wood.

7. You'll then add a little trim around the top to make it look nice, or you can leave it plain to make it look rustic. Use some small nails to attach the trim.

8. Fill it up with dirt and start planting!

Conclusion

Always remember to look for a stamp and look for HT or KD to make sure your pallet is safe. Also, be aware that colored pallets are most likely used to transport chemicals and should be avoided, especially blue and red as these were used to transport harmful chemicals. If there is any questionability about where your pallet has come from, then don't use it in your home or for garden boxes! Harmful chemicals can leach out of the wood and be sucked into plants, which you then consume.

That being said, pallets are great materials for home projects and they are very safe as long as you follow the guidelines. They're also an inexpensive way to dress up your home just the way you like it!

I hope you enjoyed this eBook on pallet projects. If you did, please leave a review at your online eBook retailer's website.

Thank you for reading!

FREE Bonus Reminder

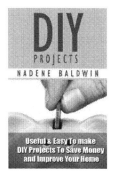

If you have not grabbed it yet, please go ahead and download your special bonus report *"DIY Projects. 13 Useful & Easy To Make DIY Projects To Save Money & Improve Your Home!"*

Simply Click the Button Below

OR **Go to This Page**

http://diyhomecraft.com/free

BONUS #2: More Free Books

Do you want to receive more Free Books?

We have a mailing list where we send out our new Books when they go free on Kindle. Click on the link below to sign up for Free Book Promotions.

=> Sign Up for Free Book Promotions <=

OR Go to this URL

http://bit.ly/1WBb1Ek

67182904R00022